Business English Study

Intermediate 7 – The Agriculture Business

Author: Paul S Fletcher

Business English Study

Intermediate 7 – The Agriculture Business

Published by BusinessEnglishStudy.com

ISBN: 9781300310990

Table of Contents

Cargill – Global Trade

- Grammar: Direct / Indirect Questions
- Listening: Cargill's Global Trade
- Functional Language: Clarification and Confirmation

Corteva Agriscience - Seeds

- Grammar: 1st & 2nd Conditional
- Listening: Global Reach
- Functional Language: Ability

Syngenta – Crop Protection

- Grammar: Present Perfect
- Listening: Company Performance
- Functional Language: Agreement and Disagreement

Claas – Farm Machinery

- Grammar: Future Tenses
- Listening: Claas Tomorrow
- Reading: Competition

Ÿnsect – Meal Worms

- Grammar: The Past Simple vs Past Continuous
- Listening: Ÿnsect today
- Functional Language: Complaints

CARGILL – Global Trade

Intermediate Level

Grammar: Direct & Indirect Question Forms

Functional Vocabulary: Clarification and Confirmation

Reading & Listening: Cargill

Pronunciation: Diphthongs /eɪ/ and /aɪ/

Cultural Awareness Point: Food Import and Export

Role-play: Do the Deal

READIING SKILLS: Cargill Incorporated

Cargill is an American multinational food corporation based in Minnetonka, Minnesota, USA.

It was founded in 1865 by William Wallace Cargill, it is the largest privately held company in the United States in terms of revenue. Cargill is a family-owned business, and the descendants of the founder own over 90% of the company.

Cargill's major businesses operations are: commodity trading, purchasing and distributing grain, palm oil; energy, steel, transport, raising livestock and food production. Cargill also has a large financial services division.

Cargill reported gross revenues of $165 billion in 2022. It last reported net profit earnings in 2021, of just below $5 billion. It employs over 160,000 workers in 66 countries, it is responsible for 25% of all United States grain  exports. The company also supplies about 22% of the United States domestic meat market, importing most of its beef products from Argentina, and is the largest poultry producer in Thailand. All the eggs used in American McDonald's restaurants pass through Cargill's plants.

Cargill's Protein Profile reported that people are eating more protein than ever before, with 61% increasing their intake in 2024. Beef, chicken and other meats are high on shopping lists, but for Millennials and Gen Z, protein goes beyond the traditional meat options and is often consumed via protein bars and shakes.

COMPREHENSION QUESTIONS

1. Who owns Cargill?
2. Cargill's major business operations are ...
3. What were profits in 2021?
4. Where does it import most of its beef from?
5. How do Millennials and Gen Z consume their protein?

GRAMMAR POINT: Direct / Indirect Questions – Polite Forms

In pairs, discuss how you can make these questions more polite:
What time is it?
Who are you?
Where is the file?
How do you know?
When exactly?

Direct and **Indirect questions** are used to ask about information we do not know.
Direct Questions – these are the normal questions we ask friends and family, plus people we know well e.g. *How much is it? What do you want?*

Indirect Questions – these are more formal and polite. We use them when talking to a person we do not know very well, or in professional situations e.g. *Could you tell me the cost please? Can I help you?*

Direct and Indirect Questions

Direct: Where is the car park?
Indirect: Could you tell me where the car park is, please?
Direct: What time does the restaurant open?
Indirect: Do you know what time the restaurant opens?
Direct: How much is it?
Indirect: I'd like to know the cost, please?
Direct: What is your name?
Indirect: May I ask your name please?

SPEAKING PRACTICE

In pairs, use Direct and Indirect questions for these situations:
1. You want to know if there is any discount.
2. The wi-fi doesn't work.
3. I want a coffee
4. Where is the toilet?
5. The food is expensive

EXERCISE: Indirect Questions: Present Simple / Past Simple

Change the direct question / request into an indirect question / request.
e.g. *Where is the farm?*
Can you tell me where the farm is, please?

1. Does he live in Paris?
2. What is this?
3. Where is the bag?
4. I want a drink.
5. What is your problem?

CULTURAL AWARENESS POINT: Meat Consumption

According to the Food & Agriculture Organisation, global meat production is expected to reach 371 million tons by next year. This growth is driven by positive numbers in Asia, especially China.

SPEAKING PRACTICE

- What meat is popular in your culture / country?
- What are the problems with high meat consumption?
- How does it impact the environment?

PRONUNCIATION PRACTICE: Diphthongs /eɪ/ and /aɪ/

A diphthong is a sound formed by the combination of two vowels in a single syllable, in which the sound begins as one vowel and moves towards another. Here are two examples:

/eɪ/ as in "play"
Starting with an "eh" sound and gliding into a brief "ee,"
Common /eɪ/ diphthong examples: *Stay - Break - They - Obey - Display*

/aɪ/ as in "light"
Starts with an open-mouthed "ah" sound and moves to a relaxed "ee" sound.
Common /aɪ/ diphthong examples: *Sky - Crying - Bright - Tied - Island*

EXERCISE: Practice pronouncing these sentences with your tutor:
- *The sky was bright at day break but the tray was light*
- *You can play in the shade but be careful of the flies*
- *She started crying when the child lied and refused to obey her*

Farming Vocabulary

A tractor is on a farm.
A harvester is on a farm.
A truck is on a farm.
A scarecrow is on a farm.
A barn is on a farm.
A wheelbarrow is on a farm.
A hay rake is on a farm.
Hay is on a farm.

SPEAKING PRACTICE – Giving Information

In pairs, take turns in spelling your name and the place where you come from to your Partner.
Partner writes down the information and repeats it back for clarification.

FUNCTIONAL VOCABULARY – Clarification and Confirmation

Understanding a guest's request and responding correctly and politely is essential. Below is a list of different ways you can make sure of understanding.

Asking For Repetition
If you don't hear what a person said
Sorry (rising intonation)
Pardon me (rising intonation)
I didn't hear that, could you repeat it please?

If you don't understand what a person said
Sorry, I don't understand
Could you say that again please, it's not clear?

Asking for Clarification
When the communication is not clear
What do you mean exactly?
Could you explain that, please?

Asking for Verification
To check you understand what a person said
You did say at 3pm, right?
It was two nights, wasn't it?
Confirming Information
To summarize the main points
Let me repeat your request
To be clear, you would like ...

Correcting Information

This is normally softened by using a polite form

Excuse me, it is not 13 but 30

Sorry, I think there is a mistake. It is 30 not 13

SPEAKING PRACTICE

In pairs, give this information to your Partner. Use the expressions of above to make sure you write down the correct information.

Student A: Role Card

My name is Jerry Granger and this is Jenny Valerian.
You can contact us on this number 07873-834-482

Student B: Role Card

My address is 40 Leicester Street, St Louis, Missouri.
My name is John Queens and my number is 07533-654-888

LISTENING: Cargill – Global Trade

FILE: https://businessenglishstudy.com/cargill-intermediate-lesson/
Or scan the QR Code for the link

> *nutrition - impact - open - billion*
> *- socially - thrive - grow - ensures*

EXERCISE: fill the gaps with the words from the box

David MacLennan, CEO of Cargill, talks about Global Trade.

.... trade responsible trade, ... that food gets from where it's grown, where it's produced, to where it's needed ....
It ensures that our customers, are ....,
are communities, ... It helps them be productive.
It creates a market for the products that they ....
In terms of economic .... the U.S department of Agriculture estimated that in 2014 the benefits to the agriculture sector from trade were $150 ....,
and a million jobs. Trade is a net job creator.
And we're asking other leaders in our industry and commodities, food and ...., to recognize the benefits of trade, to keeping the world connected, not only .... but through our trade policies.

TALKING POINT

Discuss with your Partner: What else does global trade offer? Good / Bad

ROLE-PLAY - NEGOTIATE – Agree on a Deal

In groups, discuss the pros and cons (advantages and disadvantages) of market control. Who benefits and who suffers? How can we limit the power of multinationals?

Find a Job at Cargill: https://jobs.cargill.com/

AUDIO-SCRIPT

Open trade, responsible trade, ensures that food gets from where it's grown, where it's produced, to where it's needed most.

It ensures that our customers, are farmers, are communities, thrive. It helps them be productive. It creates a market for the products that they grow.

In terms of economic impact the U.S department of Agriculture estimated that in 2014 the benefits to the agriculture sector from trade were $150 billion, and a million jobs. Trade is a net job creator.

And we're asking other leaders in our industry and commodities, food and nutrition, to recognize the benefits of trade, to keeping the world connected, not only socially but through our trade policies.

EXERCISE ANSWERS

Grammar:
1. May I ask if he lives in Paris?
2. Could you tell me what this is, please?
3. Could you tell me where she left her bag?
4. Could I have a drink please?
5. Please tell me what the problem is.

Listening Exercise: See audio-script

Reading Skills: Comprehension Questions
1. Who owns Cargill? Cargill is a family-owned business, and the descendants of the founder own over 90% of the company. What are
2. Cargill's major business operations? Commodity trading, purchasing and distributing grain, palm oil; energy, steel, transport, raising livestock and food production. Cargill also has a large financial services division
3. What were profits in 2021? Just below $5 billion
4. Where does it import most of its beef from? Argentina
5. How do Millennials and Gen Z consume their protein? It is often consumed via protein bars and shakes

CORTEVA AGRISCIENCE - Seeds

Intermediate Level

- **Grammar: First and Second Conditionals**

- **Pronunciation: Vowel Sounds**

- **Functional Language: Ability**

- **Listening: Corteva Agriscience – The Conditions**

- **Reading: Corteva Agriscience – Global Position**

- **Role Play: What to Grow on the Farm**

Agriscience is the application of Science to Agriculture.
*New breeding and seed techniques such as gene-editing create enormous
benefits: bigger plants and animals, less waste, and more disease resistance.*

SPEAKING PRACTICE: Science on the Farm
Discuss with your Partner:
The threats (dangers) of science in our food supply. How can we manage it?

FARM VOCABULARY

Write the farm words under the correct pictures -
Bucket - Fence - Seeds - Tractor - Gloves - Seeds - Sheep -
Well - Windmill - Field - Orchard - Sheep - Irrigation -
Barn - Vegetables - Wheelbarrow - Shovel and Rake -
Plant seeds - Water plants - Log - Cow

LISTENING: Corteva - Farming and Innovation

EXERCISE: fill the gaps with the words you hear

FILE: https://businessenglishstudy.com/corteva-agriscience-intermediate-lesson/
Or scan the QR Code for the link

Corteva Agriscience is creating tools to support farmers and food ....
worldwide, using scientific .... to strengthen what farming is always
done: ....
Advance seed .... to create higher yield potential, crop protection
solution to combat .... new and old, and nutrients .... to make
crops planted even more efficient. Corteva is .... to supporting
farmers around the world, through whatever challenges come their way.
Because farming is never about just one ...., and it's never about just
one ...., it's about creating sustainable solutions for decades, battling
threats that change ...., and a global food system that starts with
farming. That's why Corteva is endlessly .... new ways to support
those who support us all.

16

PRONUNCIATION: Vowel Sounds

EXERCISE: Find the words with the same vowel sound e.g. *Farm – Calm*

coach - flaw - wheat - land - sore - pants - earth - sow - green - birth

BUSINESS VOCABULARY: Trip or Travel

Discuss with your Partner: *Do you go on 'a trip' or 'a travel'?*

Trip: describes a visit to a place, there and back and usually includes a stay in the pace you visited e.g. *He is going on a business trip to Africa*

Travel: is normally used as a verb. If you travel you go to many places, or from one place to another e.g. *We travelled from Kansas to Georgia.*

EXERCISE: Fill the gaps with: Travel or Trip

1. The .... lasts 4 hours.
2. Tom ...... across the city.
3. Are you going on the ...... to Canada next year?
4. We .... to work by car.
5. We went on a .... to China last month.
6. They .... to Paris on Friday.

GRAMMAR CONDITIONALS – 1ˢᵗ and 2ⁿᵈ

Is this sentence correct? *If you will order more, I will give you a discount.*

1ˢᵀ CONDITIONAL

Situations that are probable, and you believe they will happen.

In this type of sentence, we use present simple in the *if* clause and *will/won't* plus the bare infinitive in the second clause.

> *If + present simple + will/won't + infinitive without 'to'*

e.g. *If they buy everything we will be in profit. If we sell a lot we will be rich*
The clauses can change position but **will/won't** never come in the **if** clause
If you come I will show you (is correct)
If you will come I will show you (is incorrect)

2ⁿᵈ CONDITIONAL

Situations that are possible but highly unlikely, and you don't believe they will happen.

In this type of sentence we use the past simple in the *if* clause and *would/not (or could/not)* plus the bare infinitive in the second clause.

> *If + past simple + would/not (could/not) + infinitive without 'to'*

e.g. *If I won the lottery I would buy a house.*
The clauses can change position, but *'**would**'* never comes in the *'if'* clause

If I had to I would work on a farm (**correct**)

If I would have to I would work on a farm (**incorrect**)

EXERCISE: Put the verbs into 1st or 2nd conditional

1. If John (not decide) .... soon, the opportunity ...... (disappear).

2. If I ...... (meet) the boss I ...... (tell) him the problem I have.

3. Paul .... (earn) a lot of money if he ...... (sell) all the products.

4. I .... (say) yes if Coteva........... (offer) me the job.

5. If I .... (walk) the 8 miles to work I .... (save) money.

6. When you .... (drink) whisky you .... (get) drunk.

7. If this skirt .... (fit) me it .... (be) a miracle.

8. What .... you (do) if your boss .... (offer) you promotion?

9. What .... you (buy) if you .... (win) the lottery?

10. We .... (sell) more animals when we .... (have) a promotion.

FUNCTIONAL LANGUAGE PRACTICE - Ability and Inability

Make Able / Possible	Be Able	Make unable / impossible	Be Unable to / impossible
Enable	Can	Prohibit	Can't
Allow	Be able to	Prevent from	Be impossible to
Permit	Be capable of	Stop/halt	Unable to
Approved	Be possible to	Forbidden	Be incapable of

Example Sentences

- *Leaders can delegate and motivate*
- *The truck is <u>unable to</u> depart tomorrow*

1. **Ability:**
   Making someone able **or something** possible
   The computer system <u>enables</u> Coteva <u>to</u> change orders quickly

2. **Being able**
   <u>Corteva is able</u> to support a lot of farmers

3. **Making something impossible or something unable**
   Slow production <u>prevents</u> the competition <u>from</u> growing.

Uses

- **Being able to do something:**
Great businessmen <u>are capable of</u> inspiring others

- **Making something impossible or someone unable:**
The high cost <u>prevented us from</u> growing olives
The manager <u>stopped</u> the meeting early

- **Being unable to do something:**
I want to visit the factory but <u>I can't</u> (something is preventing me)

20

EXERCISE: Fill the gaps with an appropriate verb from the table above and put it in the correct form. More than one answer is possible.

1. Yesterday, we .... enter the shop but today we .... (be un/able).
2. The price .... us .... making tractors in England (prevent).
3. Apologies, we are .... complete the order (impossible).
4. The staff were .... work at the weekend (possible).

SPEAKING PRACTICE - Ability

With your Partner, discuss your ability or inability to become a successful farmer. Ask each other questions.

READING: Corteva Agriscience

Corteva Agriscience is a major American agricultural chemical and seed company. It has a presence in more than 140 countries, and generated $17 billion in net sales in 2024.
Corteva Agriscience has more than 150 research and development facilities specialising in seed and pesticides, and has patents on more than 65 active ingredients.
The name Corteva comes from a combination of words meaning 'heart' and 'nature.'

Key points about Corteva Agriscience in 2025:

Commitment to Food Security and Sustainability: Corteva remains dedicated to addressing the world's food security challenges and promoting sustainable agricultural practices.
Focus on Innovation: Corteva is introducing new soybean herbicides like Kyber Pro and Sonic Boom.
Financial Performance: Share value is between $2.70 and $2.95, which is lower than expected.
Collaboration: Corteva is actively collaborating with organizations like Gates Agricultural Innovations to accelerate agri-innovation.
Global Operations: Corteva operates globally and is therefore impacted by currency fluctuations and market conditions.

COMPREHENSION QUESTIONS

1. How many countries does Corteva operate in?
2. What research does it specialise in?
3. What new products are being introduced?
4. How is its financial performance?
5. What impacts Corteva on a global level?

ROLE-PLAY: What to Grow on the Farm

In pairs / groups, decide what you want to grow on your small farm. Decide on the location of the farm.

Top 5 Most Profitable Small Farm Crops

1. Gourmet Mushrooms (Oyster and Shiitake)
2. Salad greens
3. Heirloom Tomatoes
4. Garlic
5. Strawberries

Consider these points
- **Market Demand:** Research what high value crops are in demand locally and regionally.
- **Growing Conditions:** Matching your crops to your climate and soil conditions is essential.
- **Initial Investment vs. Long-Term Gains:** Certain crops require a higher initial investment for seeds, specialized equipment, or infrastructure.
- **Labour and Resource Requirements:** Consider the ongoing labour and resources needed to cultivate each crop.

Apply for a job at Corteva: https://www.corteva.co.uk/who-we-are/internships.html

....

AUDIO-SCRIPT

Corteva Agriscience is creating tools to support farmers and food security worldwide, using scientific breakthroughs to strengthen what farming is always done: persevere.
Advance seed breeding to create higher yield potential, crop protection solution to combat threats new and old, and nutrients maximisers to make crops planted even more efficient. Corteva is devoted to supporting farmers around the world, through whatever challenges come their way. Because farming is never about just one hurdle, and it's never about just one harvest, it's about creating sustainable solutions for decades, battling threats that change continuously, and a global food system that starts with farming. That's why Corteva is endlessly innovating new ways to support those who support us all.

EXERCISE ANSWERS

FARM VOCABULARY
well, vegetables, cow, fence, orchard, irrigation, seeds, field, barn, wheelbarrow, windmill, log, gloves, plant seeds, sheep, tractor, hay, bucket, water plants, and shovel and rake

LISTENING EXERCISE: See audio-script

GRAMMAR EXERCISE: Put the verbs into 1st or 2nd conditional
1. If John doesn't decide soon, the opportunity will disappear.
2. If I met the boss, I would tell him the problem I have.
3. Paul will earn a lot of money if he sells all the products.
4. I would say yes if Coteva offered me the job.
5. If I walked the 8 miles to work, I would save money.
6. When you drink whisky, you get drunk.
7. If this skirt fits me, it will be a miracle.
8. What would you do if your boss offered you promotion?
9. What would you buy if you won the lottery?
10. We sell more animals when we have a promotion.

BUSINESS VOCABULARY
1. The <u>travel</u> time is 4 hours.
2. Tom <u>travels</u> across the city.
3. Are you going on the <u>trip</u> to Canada next year?
4. We <u>travel</u> to work by car.
5. We went on a <u>trip</u> to China last month.
6. They will <u>travel</u> to Paris on Friday.

PRONUNCIATION
coach – sow
flaw – sore
wheat – green

land – pants
earth - birth

ABILITY/INABILITY

1. Yesterday, we were unable to enter the shop but today we could.
2. The price prevents us from making tractors in England.
3. Apologies, we are unable to complete the order.
4. The staff were able to work at the weekend.

READING EXERCISE - COMPREHENSION QUESTIONS

1. How many countries does Corteva operate in? 140
2. What research does it specialise in? Seed and pesticides, with patents on more than 65 active ingredients.
3. What new products are being introduced? Soybean herbicides like Kyber Pro and Sonic Boom.
4. How is its financial performance? Share value is between $2.70 and $2.95, which is lower than expected.
5. What impacts Corteva on a global level? Currency fluctuations and market conditions

SYGENTA – Crop Protection

Intermediate Level

Grammar: Present Perfect

Functional Vocabulary: Agreement / Disagreement

Listening: Sygenta

Pronunciation: Hard or Soft /g/

Reading: Sygenta Origins

Cultural Awareness: Health and Safety

Role-play: Enquiries: Go Organic?

SPEAKING PRACTICE: Syngenta Global AG is a global agricultural technology company headquartered in Basel, Switzerland. It covers crop protection and seeds for farmers. Syngenta is part of the Syngenta Group, which is owned by Sinochem, a Chinese state-owned company.

Discuss: In pairs, ask each other these questions
- Have you heard of Sygenta?
- How long have you lived in this city?
- Have you ever been to China?
- Have you studied the Present Perfect before?

GRAMMAR PRACTICE: Present Perfect Simple

	Positive	Negative	Question
I / you / we / they	*I have spoken.*	*I have not spoken.*	*Have I spoken?*
he / she / it	*He has spoken.*	*He has not spoken.*	*Has he spoken?*

Use of Present Perfect

- Puts emphasis on the result e.g. she *has worked* here for 10 years
- Action that starts in the past and is not finished e.g. the meeting *has* not *finished*
- Action that recently finished e.g. he *has just finished* the interview
- Finished action that has an influence on the present e.g. I *have lost* my phone.

Action that has taken place once, never or several times before the moment of speaking, when the time is not important e.g. I *have never been* to Scotland.

Signal Words of Present Perfect

These words indicate that the present perfect is used in this sentence.

already, ever, just, never, yet, not yet, so far, till now, up to now

EXERCISES

1. Write the participle forms of the following verbs.

make →

see →

catch →

have →

buy →

2. Complete the table in present perfect simple.

Positive	Negative	Question
He has begun.		
		Has she eaten?
		Have you been to Paris?
Tina has tried.		
	They have not gone	

3. Write sentences in present perfect simple.
1. we / take / chances –
2. our team / lose / the competition –
3. she / find / the solution –
4. they / not / learn / the lesson –
5. Rachel / speak / to Paul –

4. Write questions in present perfect simple.
1. you / send / the email –
2. the manager / go / the meeting –
3. she / buy / a new computer –
4. they / sell / the building –
5. Susan / wear / yet / the jacket –

LISTENING SKILLS – Syngenta's New Logo

FILE: https://businessenglishstudy.com/syngenta-intermediate-lesson/
Or scan the QR Code for the link

EXERCISE: Fill the gaps with words you hear:

The new Syngenta group .... connects to our businesses.
It moves us into the future with .... new colours, representing the ....,
..............., and .... of the four seasons.
Like the four points of a ...., guiding all we do.
The elements that together create the conditions for .... in all four
corners of the world.
And giving us an identity that will transform everything it ....
Something truly world class.
Drawing on the .... of our businesses and brands.
Helping them to ....
Together we ....
Together we are Syngenta group.

TALKING POINT: Logos

With your Partner, think of other famous logos and discuss what they represent.
Present your ideas to the rest of the class.

SPEAKING PRACTICE: Organic versus Conventional Farming

Organic is different from conventional farming because it only uses natural processes and bans (or restricts) the use of chemical support e.g. pesticides and fertilisers. Conventional farming uses a lot of chemical products to maximize crop and animal yields.

DISCUSS: The pros and cons (advantages and disadvantages) of organic and conventional farming.

PRONUNCIATION PRACTICE: /g/

The letter "g" can be pronounced as either a hard "g" (like in "go") or a soft "g" (like in "gem").
The pronunciation depends on the letter that follows the "g".
A hard "g" occurs when the "g" is followed by the vowels "a," "o," or "u," or by a consonant.
A soft "g" (like a "J" sound) usually occurs when the "g" is followed by the letters "e" "i" or "y

Hard	Soft
Garbage	Gentle

EXERCISE: Pronounce the words and put in the hard or soft /G/ box:

Gist, Giant, Gym, Genre
Go, Gum, Ginger, Grad,
Glue, General, Gyp, Age,
Goat, Girl, Magic, Great,
Glove, Green, Gem, Group.

BUSINESS SKILLS - Expressing Agreement/Disagreement

Some phrases you can use:

Stating your opinion	In my opinion... According to Susan... As far as I'm concerned... If you ask me... The way I see it... If you want my honest opinion....
Asking for an opinion	What do you think? Do you agree? Wouldn't you say? How do you feel about that? Do you have anything to say about this?
Expressing agreement	I agree with you 100 percent. I couldn't agree with you more. That's so true. You're absolutely right. That's exactly how I feel. Exactly / Absolutely / Definitely (weak) I suppose so / I guess so. You have a point there.
Expressing disagreement	I don't think so. (strong) No way. I'm afraid I disagree. (strong) I totally disagree. That's not always true. That's not always the case.
Interruptions	Can I add something here? Sorry to interrupt, but...
Settling an argument	Let's leave it, shall we? I think we're going to have to agree to disagree.

SPEAKING PRACTICE:

In pairs, discuss these topics. Agree and disagree with your partner.

- Farms need to be big to make economic sense
- You can make a lot of profit from the restricting supply
- Hormones are good. They increase animal size and profits

CULTURAL AWARENESS POINT: Holistic Pest Control

Holistic pest control focuses on prevention and minimizing the use of pesticides. It involves understanding the pest's biology, the environment it lives in, to develop a friendly solution. Several countries use holistic pest control. Examples include countries within the European Union, such as Luxembourg and Germany, who have banned pesticides on public land.

With your Partner discuss: Is holistic pest control a thing for the rich and industrialised cheap food made for the poor? What is the future?

READING SKILLS: Syngenta and AI

EXERCISE: Read and dd a paragraph title from the box to the key 5 points

> **Pest Control - R&D (research and development) - the Field - Farmers' Hands - Supply Chain Management)**

In 2025, Syngenta CEO, Jeff Rowe, presented five key trends in artificial intelligence that will impact agriculture.

"AI and digital tools are revolutionizing farming practices," he explained. "Advanced monitoring systems integrate satellite imagery, drones, and soil maps, to enable precise crop management. Predictive analytics, powered by AI and machine learning, transform re-active practices into pro-active strategies."

The five key points for Syngenta and AI

1. **AI in ....:** Syngenta uses machine learning programmes to identify the best ingredients for synthetic and biological products.
2. **AI in ....:** AI-driven systems monitor and predict soil health.
3. **AI in ....:** AI tools act as an agronomic advisor to help farmers decide on the best crop decisions.
4. **AI in ....:** AI helps farmers target crop protection in the infested areas only. No need to spray everything.
5. **AI in...........................:** Forecasting, market prediction, and the reduction of waste will improve efficiency.

ROLE-PLAY – AI in Agriculture

In pairs, Think of other applications for AI in agriculture and present to the class. Take Questions.

Find a Job at Syngenta: https://www.syngenta.co.uk/careers

AUDIO-SCRIPT

The new Syngenta group logo connects to our businesses.
It moves us into the future with fresh new colours, representing the vibrancy, wonder and abundance of the four seasons.
Like the 4 points of a compass, guiding all we do.
The elements that together create the conditions for growth in all four corners of the world.
And giving us an identity that will transform everything it touches
Something truly world class.
Drawing on the strengths of our businesses and brands.
Helping them to thrive.
Together we grow.
Together we are Syngenta group.

EXERCISE ANSWERS

Listening: See Audio-Script

GRAMMAR Exercise 1:
1. make → made
2. see → seen
3. catch → caught
4. have → had
5. buy → bought

Exercise 2.

Positive	Negative	Question
He has begun.	He has not begun	Has he begun?
She has eaten	She has not eaten.	Has she eaten?
You have been to Paris	You have not been to Paris	Have you been to Paris?
Tina has tried.	Tina has not tried	Has Tina tried?
They have gone	They have not gone	Have they gone?

Exercise 3.
1. We have taken chances
2. Our team has lost the competition
3. She has found the solution
4. They have not learnt / learned the lesson
5. Rachel has spoken to Paul

Exercise 4.
1. Have you sent the email?

34

2. Has the manager gone to the meeting?
3. Has she bought a new computer?
4. Have they sold the building?
5. Has Susan worn the jacket yet?

PRONUCIATION

HARD: Go, Gum, Goat, Girl, Great, Glove, Green, Group, Grad, Glue.

SOFT: Gem, Giant, Gist, Gym, Genre, Ginger, General, Gyp, Age, Magic.

READING:

1. R&D (research and development)
2. The Field
3. Farmers' Hands
4. Pest Control
5. Supply Chain Management

CLAAS – Farm Machinery

Intermediate Level

- Grammar: Future Tenses

- Pronunciation: Spot the Homophones

- Functional Vocabulary: Machinery Vocabulary

- Listening: CLAAS Competition

- Reading: CLAAS Background

- Role Play: Buy a New Tractor

SPEAKING PRACTICE: Discuss these questions with a partner

- *Which tractor accessory is important on a wheat farm?*
- *What other machines are needed on a wheat farm?*

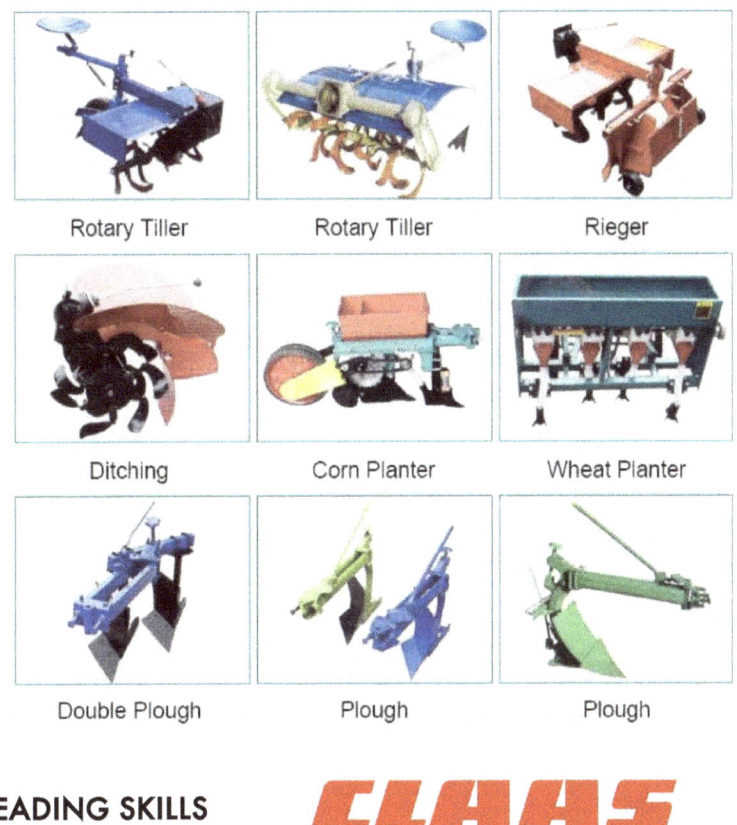

Rotary Tiller	Rotary Tiller	Rieger
Ditching	Corn Planter	Wheat Planter
Double Plough	Plough	Plough

READING SKILLS ***CLAAS***

EXERCISE: put the correct a preposition into the gaps

CLAAS is an agricultural machinery manufacturer based .... Germany. It was founded .... 1913 .... August Claas, CLAAS is a family business and a market leader.

It's product range includes tractors, balers, mowers, rakes, combine harvesters, and is investing heavily .... farming information technology. CLAAS employs around 11,500 employees worldwide and reported a turnover .... €5 billion .... 2024.

About 80% of sales are generated outside .... Germany.

PRONUNCIATION PRACTICE: Homophones

Homophones are words (or combinations of words), which sound the same, but are spelt differently and have different meanings, e.g. *too, to* and *two.*

EXERCISE: find the 5 pairs of homophones in the list below.

Hair - Bare - Site – Here - Peace - Poor - Pure - Air - Sit - Foot - Peas - Work - Thought - Walk - Beer - Ear - Sight - Piece - Pour - Bear - Hear – Fort - Pair

FUNCTIONAL VOCABULARY: The Role of the Combine Harvester

This is a machine used to harvest a variety of grain crops. It "combines" many tasks including cutting, threshing, and discarding the waste.

Season Used: Harvest

Reaping: The process of cutting and collecting the mature grain.

Threshing: The process of separating the grain from the straw and chaff, which is necessary to prepare the grain for storage or further processing.

Leaving Cover: The combine spreads out non usable parts of the plants (stem, leaves) onto the field so they can be turned into nutrients for next year's crop.

GRAMMAR PRACTICE: Review of The Future Tenses

1. **Prediction: WILL**
   Based on forecasts yields will grow by 5% next year.

2. **Future Fact: WILL**
   The service contract will finish on Monday the 5th.
   The new import regulations will take effect in June.

3. **Promises & Assurances: WILL**
   The company will do its best to complete the order by tomorrow.

4. **Spontaneous Decisions for the Future: WILL**
   Is there a complaint? I'll speak to the customer.

5. **Intentions & Plans: GOING TO**
   She's going to check the delivery system tomorrow.
   • **Going to** is also used for a future based on present evidence:
   When you consider his diplomacy, he is going to go far in the company.
   • **Going to** suggests determination:
   We're going to sell a lot more cars this year than we did last year.

6. **Future Plans: PRESENT CONTINUOUS**
   I'm having lunch with the CEO tomorrow
   Where are you signing the contract, Paris or Rome?

EXERCISE: Choose the correct form of the verb for the gaps

1. I've decided to raise some money. I .... (sell) some shares.
2. He's exhausted. If he's not careful .... (have) a nervous breakdown.
3. CLAAS.................. (do) its best to complete the order by tomorrow.
4. The plan is, we .... (buy) the company next month.
5. The team .... (go) to Hamburg tomorrow. It's in the diary.

READING SKILLS 2: CLAAS Future Plans

Here's a more detailed look at CLAAS's future plans:

1. Digital Solutions and Connectivity:
CLAAS is expanding its digital platform, CLAAS Connect, to provide more connectivity and smarter machines.

2. Plant Modernization and Expansion:
CLAAS is investing in extensive modernization projects at its plants, including the ForageGO!

3. Autonomous Technology:
CLAAS is actively developing and integrating autonomous technologies into its machinery, including tractors, Agbots, implements, and drones. CLAAS envisions a future where machine combinations can operate autonomously, requiring less operator intervention.

4. Sustainability and Efficiency:
CLAAS is exploring the use of sustainable liquid fuels like HVO (Hydrotreated Vegetable Oil) to reduce carbon emissions.

5. Collaboration and Partnerships:
CLAAS collaborates with partners like AgXeed to explore and develop autonomous technologies

COMPREHENSION EXERCISE

Answer these questions. NOTE: they are not in chronological order.

1. What autonomous technologies is CLAAS integrating?
2. What modernisation project is CLAAS investing in?
3. What can HVO do?
4. Who is CLAAS partnering with?
5. What does CLAAS Connect do?
6. What does CLAAS see the future as?

VOCABULARY OF THE FARM

EXERCISE: match the words (1-7) with their meaning (A-G)

1.	Acre	=	A. enclose
2.	Arable	=	B. roll of hay
3.	Hay	=	C. least expensive
4.	Bale	=	D. dry grass for animal feed
5.	Wrap	=	E. land size of 4,045 square metres
6.	Back-up	=	F. support
7.	Cheapest	=	G. crop land

LISTENING SKILLS: CLAAS Farmer

FILE: https://businessenglishstudy.com/claas-intermediate-lesson/
Or scan the QR Code for the link

EXERCISE: Listen and fill in the gaps with words from Farm Vocabulary

Hi my name is Jeff Thomas. Me and Rhod, my son, farm and contract here in West Wales
We're farming about 250, 260 .... with beef, sheep and ....
The biggest part of the business is baling, and we .... and ....
somewhere between 20 and 25,000 .... a year.
We buy the CLAAS product basically because, whilst it's not the ....
it's the best value for money, as well as that the backup we get from our local dealer is second to none.

ROLE-PLAY: Buy a Tractor

In pairs / groups, choose a tractor to buy for your medium size potato farm. You have a maximum of $300,000 to spend. Discuss your needs and budget.

Mahindra 475 Series - $100,000 minimum
Specifically designed for potato farming. It has precise hydraulics for sowing / digging. Contains basic technology.

John Deere 6250R - $200,000 minimum
A powerful and lightweight option, suitable for larger potato farms. It offers advanced technology.

Claas Arion 610.- $150,000 minimum
Provides high horsepower and the best technology, making it suitable for a variety of applications on larger farms.

Find a Job at Claas: https://www.claas.com/en-gb/career/jobs

AUDIO-SCRIPT

Hi my name is Jeff Thomas. Me and Rhod, my son, farm and contract here in West Wales
We're farming about 250, 260 acres with beef, sheep and arable.
The biggest part of the business is baling, and we bale and wrap somewhere between 20 and 25,000 bales a year.
We buy the CLAAS product basically because, whilst it's not the cheapest it's the best value for money, as well as that the backup we get from our local dealer is second to none.

EXERCISE ANSWERS

READING EXERCISE 1:

in – in - by – in – of – in - of

PRONUNCIATION:

1.Bare – Bear 2. Site – Sight 3. Here – Hear 4. Peace – Piece 5. Poor - Pour

GRAMMAR EXERCISE -EXERCISE

1. I've decided to raise some money. I am going to sell some shares.
2. He's exhausted. If he's not careful is going to have a nervous breakdown.
3. CLAAS will do its best to complete the order by tomorrow.
4. We are going to buy the company next month.
5. The team is going to Hamburg tomorrow. It's in the diary.

READING EXERCISE 2:

1. What autonomous technologies is CLAAS integrating? Tractors, Agbots, implements, and drones.
2. What modernisation project is CLAAS investing in? ForageGO!
3. What can HVO do? Reduce carbon emissions
4. Who is CLAAS partnering with? AgXeed
5. What does CLAAS Connect do? It provides more connectivity and smarter machines.
6. What does CLAAS see the future as? Machine combinations that an operate autonomously, requiring less operator intervention

Vocabulary of the Farm

1. Acres   =   land size of 4,045 square metres
2. Arable   =   crop land
3. Hay   =   dry grass for animal feed
4. Bale   =   roll of hay
5. Wrap   =   enclose
6. Back-up   =   support
7. Cheapest   =   least expensive

LISTENING EXERCISE: See audio script

Ÿnsect – Meal Worms

Intermediate Level

Reading: **Ÿnsect – The Origins**

Grammar: **Past Simple and Past Continuous**

Functional Vocabulary: **Comments and Complaints**

Pronunciation: **Word Stress**

Cultural Awareness: **Eating Insects**

Listening: **Ÿnsect Today**

Role Play: **Production Cost Issues**

SPEAKING PRACTICE: Discuss these questions with a partner:
What do you know about mealworms? What can we do with them?

READING – ŸNSECT'S MEAL WORMS

Mealworms, the larvae of the flour beetle, are used as a food source for various animals, including birds, reptiles, fish, and even some small mammals. They are also a sustainable food source for humans and can be used as a protein supplement in various foods.

In 2011, Ÿnsect was created in France by 4 scientists, whose aim was to bring mealworms into the food chain.

The aggrotech industry has promoted Ÿnsect as one of the most dynamic start-ups in Europe, but there have been problems. According to news reports in 2025, Ÿnsect faced financial difficulties and the company needed to restructure to avoid bankruptcy. The search for new investors has so far been unsuccessful so Ÿnsect plans to move its annual production of 3 trillion mealworms out of France and into Asia. A company spokesperson said: *The climate is wrong in Europe. The cost of production is too high, due to labour and energy expenses. The health and safety regulations in the EU are over protective.*

COMPREHENSION QUESTIONS

1. What are mealworms used for?
2. Who started Ÿnsect?
3. How many mealworms does Ÿnsect produce each year?
4. What are the problems with producing in Europe for Ÿnsect?

SPEAKING PRACTICE

In pairs, discuss humans eating insects. What are the pros and cons (advantages and disadvantages)?

SELECTED EXPRESSIONS

EXERCISE: match the expression (1-6) with its meaning (a-f)

1. Hands on   -   a. opposite
2. Run of the mill   -   b. provide service
3. One off   -   c. ordinary
4. Cater for   -   d. investigate
5. Check out   -   e. actively connected
6. Visa-versa   -   f. happens once only

PRONUNCIATION: Stress Patterns

In English, we give stress to certain words while other words are unstressed.

EXERCISE: Say these words using the highlighted stress patterns

TERRible – inCREDible - braZIL - jaPAN - BerLIN - TOURist - PHOtograph oCCAsion – eFFIcient - reVIEW - reFER – sufficient - REFerence - eSSENtial - caREER - COffee – iDEa - perMISSion - hoTEL - eQUALity - adVANtage –

46

LISTENING SKILLS: ŸNSECT

FILE: https://businessenglishstudy.com/ynsect-intermediate-lesson/
Or scan the QR Code for the link

EXERCISE: fill the gaps with the words you hear

*Founded in 2011, in Paris France by scientists and ....
.... Ÿnsect is the world leader natural insect ingredients to feed
............, ..., and ....*

*By .... we need to increase our food production by .... to meet
the need of people globally. And this with only .... extra arable land
available.*

*The company, a certified B Corp, provides a healthy natural and sustainable
alternative protein that uses .... less land and .... few resources
than traditional livestock farming.*

*Ÿnsect is established in France, ..., and also in the ...., with
the integration in .... of Protifarm, a leading player in insect ingredients
for human applications.*

Ask your Partner: Is this sentence correct? *I was making lots of money so I bought a holiday home.*

GRAMMAR REVIEW: The Past Simple and Past Continuous

The Past Simple Tense
FORM: I was – I worked – I wrote
This tense is formed using the past simple tense of the verb.

When to use the PAST SIMPLE
Completed Action in the Past. Use the Simple Past to express the idea that an action started and finished at a specific time in the past.
E.g. *I saw the presentation last week. I didn't see the manager yesterday.*

The Past Continuous Tense
FORM: I was writing – I wasn't listening – Were you working late?
This tense is formed using two components: the verb: *to be* (in the past tense), and the *-ing* form of a verb.

When to use the PAST CONTINUOUS
- The past continuous is used when one action began before another, and finished after it. For example:
  I was working when he arrived. I started working (at 8 p.m.), then he arrived (at 9 p.m.), then I finished working (at 10 p.m.).

- We can also use the past continuous tense to describe TWO actions that were BOTH continuing at the same time in the past. In this case, we use the past continuous for both actions: *While I was reading, she was working.*

EXERCISE: Select the correct tense for each gap.

1. When Jane ....(leave) the farm, she .... (meet) the owner
2. Jack .... (arrive) London yesterday. Last week he ...... (work) in Brazil.
3. What .... you .... (do) during the presentation? .... you .... (listen)?
4. I .... (receive) the figures yesterday. The manager .... (give) them to me.
5. Trevor .... (talk) while the chef .... (prepare) the food.

48

SPEAKING PRACTICE:

In pairs, describe the worst meal you have ordered in a restaurant.
Use the past simple and past continuous when talking about the events.

CULTURAL AWARENESS POINT: Complaining

In the UK, the style is not to complain in public but to suffer in silence. This because the British do not like confrontation. They prefer to say everything is OK and then go home and complain to their friends or on-line.

SPEAKING PRACTICE: In pairs, discuss how you complain in your country / culture. How you complain as a person. How do you feel when you complain? Is it better to say nothing and complain later or confront the problem immediately?

FUNCTIONAL VOCABULARY: Comments and Complaints

What is the difference between a comment and a complaint?
Comments are when you give your opinion of something – good or bad.
Complaints are words of displeasure in response to an action or situation.

Discuss: Do you ever complain? What do you complain about?

Complaining - Here are some expressions you can use when complaining:

I have a complaint to make ...
Sorry to bother you but ...
I'm sorry to say this but ...
I'm afraid there is a problem with ...
Excuse me but there is a problem about ...
I want to complain about ...
I'm angry about ...

RESPONDING TO COMPLAINTS

Positive response to complaints:
I'm so sorry, but this will never happen again.
I'm sorry, we promise never to make the same mistake again.
I'm really sorry; we'll do our utmost/best not to do the same mistake again.

Negative response to complaints:
Sorry, but there is nothing we can do about it.
I'm afraid, there isn't much we can do about it.
Everybody else thinks the food is fine.

Things to remember about complaints:
When expressing a complaint in English, it helps to be polite. Although **"I'm angry about the eggs. They taste disgusting,"** is one way of expressing a complaint, it sounds rude.

SPEAKING EXERCISE: Complaining

In pairs, take turns to complain about:

1. The insect menu

2. The noise of the construction site

3. The farm machine does not work

4. The bad service of the sales staff

5. The additional charges on the bill

ROLE-PLAY: Insect Menu

In smalls groups, create an insect menu that includes new dishes and
ingredients e.g. worm soup with bee kebab
Present the menu to other students who are customers in your restaurant.
Take their order.
Use the past simple and continuous tense in your presentation.

Find a Job at Ÿnsect: https://www.linkedin.com/company/ynsect/jobs/

AUDIO-SCRIPT

Founded in 2011, in Paris France by scientists and environmental activists, Ÿnsect is the world leader natural insect ingredients to feed animals, plants, and humans.
By 2050 we need to increase our food production by 70% to meet the need of people globally. And this with only 5% extra arable land available.
The company, a certified B Corp, provides a healthy natural and sustainable alternative protein that uses 98% less land and 50% few resources than traditional livestock farming.
Ÿnsect is established in France, the USA, and also in the Netherlands, with the integration in 2021 of Protifarm, a leading player in insect ingredients for human applications.

EXERCISE ANSWERS

SELECTED EXPRESSIONS
1. Hands on   -   a. actively connected
2. Run of the mill   -   b. ordinary
3. One off   -   c. happens once only
4. Cater for   -   d. provide service
5. Check out   -   e. investigate
6. Visa-versa   -   f. opposite

READING EXERCISE:
1. A food source for birds, reptiles, fish, and some small mammals. They are also a sustainable food source for humans and can be used as a protein supplement in various foods.
2. 4 Scientists in France
3. 3 trillion
4. The climate is wrong. The cost of production is too high, due to labour and energy expenses. The health and safety regulations in the EU are over protective.

GRAMMAR:
1. When Jane <u>was leaving</u> the farm, she <u>met</u> the owner.
2. Jack <u>arrived</u> London yesterday. Last week he <u>was working</u> in Brazil.
3. What <u>were</u> you <u>doing</u> during the presentation? <u>Were</u> you <u>listening</u>?
4. I <u>received</u> the figures yesterday. The manager <u>gave</u> them to me.
5. Trevor <u>was talking</u> while the chef <u>prepared</u> the food.

LISTENING SKILLS: See Audio Script